Breathing Between the Lines: Poems

Camino del Sol

A Chicana and Chicano

Literary Series

# BREATHING

# BETWEEN

# THE LINES

POEMS

Demetria Martínez

THE UNIVERSITY OF ARIZONA PRESS   Tucson

The University of Arizona Press
© 1997 Demetria Martínez
∞ This book is printed on acid-free, archival-quality paper.
Manufactured in the United States of America
10   09   08   07   06   05      7 6 5 4 3 2
Library of Congress Cataloging-in-Publication Data
Martínez, Demetria, 1960–
Breathing between the lines : poems / Demetria Martínez.
p.   cm. – (Camino del sol)
ISBN-13: 978-0-8165-1798-5 (paper : acid-free paper)—
ISBN-10: 0-8165-1798-3
ISBN-13: 978-0-8165-1796-1 (cloth : acid-free paper)—
ISBN-10: 0-8165-1796-7
1. Mexican American women—Poetry. I. Title. II. Series.
PS3563.A7333337B7  1997
811'.54—dc21   96-45808

Some of the poems in this volume were published previously
in *River Styx, The Massachusetts Review, Enclitic, Crossroads,* and in the
anthologies *Skin Deep: Women Writing on Color, Culture and Identity*
and *Paper Dance: 55 Latino Poets.*

The epigraph on page vii was excerpted from the poem "IV.
Ice Horses" in *She Had Some Horses,* © 1982 by Joy Harjo, re-
printed with permission of the publisher, Thunder's Mouth
Press.

to my friends, this is
the letter i had no time
to write, with love

Thus saith the Lord God unto these bones;
Behold, I will cause breath to enter into you,
and ye shall live. —Ezekiel 37:5


These are the ones who escape
after the last hurt is turned inward;
they are the most dangerous ones.
—Joy Harjo, *She Had Some Horses*

# Contents

*Gracias a mis familias, Márquez y Martínez,*
*para todos los libros y todos los sueños.*
*Estos cantos son para ustedes.*

I wish to thank the community at the
William Joiner Center for the Study of War
and Social Consequences, University of
Massachusetts, Boston. Most of these poems
were begun there in June 1995. They were
completed the following month at La Casita
in Jemez Springs, New Mexico, thanks to
the hospitality of Rudolfo and Pat Anaya.

# I. CODE TALKERS

## Untitled

Mystical?
Too clinical.
God?
The name has been
smoked down
to a stub.

For sixteen years
I have ransacked
the universe,
unsealing files,
lifting lyrics,
looking for a way
to say how it was.

Because we have
no word for light
we live in shadows.

# Milagros*

*after a painting by Francisco LeFebre*

When at last you find something worth
longing for

you breed horses again
half Peruvian paso, half Arabian
dance step and a mane like Rapunzel

grinding hummingbird bones
to a powder, aphrodisiac from before Columbus
your brushes on fire with color

and me? I listen for words that mean *heart*,
collect them like *milagros* we pin
to statues of saints
in the church at Magdalena

because we are beyond wishing
folding prayers like paper airplanes

no, the time has come to storm heaven
until the gods weep at the sight
of the horses' bare backs

and become flesh, and ride
and ride and ride

---

*A *milagro*, which means "miracle" in Spanish, depicts the object
for which a miracle is sought, such as a broken leg or money
to buy a house.

# Night

Because we cannot be together
we live in six notes of Vietnamese
where no one can understand
us except those who speak
in tongues and the language of birds

Because we cannot be together
we boil the roots of telephone cords torn
from the black soils of sleep
hold negatives up to the light
in houses where windows
are yellow eyes, our power
pirated from street lamps
and flooding gutters

So many years since that chopstick
click of yes, so many years I can count them
in illegal U.S. wars, pueblo feast days
wicks drowned in red wax

These are the ruined
scripts of what might
have been an ordinary life

These are the monuments

The right to remain

Breathing between the lines

## The Dress Daisy * Gave Me

1.
Flaming sunflowers

Fire of red and gold mouths,
mouths and tongues

the end of Somoza began
as whispers against Somoza

a plan, a plan and a song

notes ascending until the lie shattered

turning wine into water,
water into crops

2.
She tells me
the most unlikely soils
give way to love,
stems and seeds

and that the most unlikely love
begins as a dream
of rice and oil and the shriek
of onions

the setting out of plates

a spray of green elephants
on Indian cotton

hanging in the doorway to another room

3.
I feel the flaming mouths
against my bare skin

I wear this for you
though you cannot see me

It might be years
before our fingers curl together

in my heat like these leaves
Years

4.
The sunflower dress
hangs on a hook
as I take the receiver
from its cradle

The end of our solitude
began in whispers

dreams cracking open like shells

seeds, salt on our lips

dreams opening

like the fist of an infant

\*Nicaraguan poet Daisy Zamora was a
combatant of the national Sandinista
Liberation Front and served as vice
minister of culture after the 1979 revolution.

## Before You

My poems had no you
No eye
of a needle
to pass through
No hot
coals over
which to walk

Nine lives
Sacred heart
Red nails
Lips open
to the whys of the world

Before you, nothing

I pin these poems
on you like stars,
tattoo tears

Where you go, these words
go, forever
my suitcase ready at the door

## Everywoman

Any minute I will be

bloody as a beet

As the blade of
a Toltec

Help me

All I want
is a clean house

Salsa on Muenster cheese
*Pan dulce*

Please

Say something

salty and sweet
Say something

to make me cry
I will abuse you

Then use you
A happy woman

Melon-heavy

Ready for your thump

## History

We prayed for rain
and the rain came.

Squash, beans,
chiles, corn.

New World

Seeds from before
the time of Christ.

Feasting before a fire
we stole from your lover's camp.

## Code Talkers

How
long
must
we
live
in
codes
only
the
Navajo
can
break?
How
long
will
two
tin
cans
conceal
hearts
before
the
string

snaps?

## We Talk About Spanish

Not in Spanish
Dream with dictionaries
Blood-thinners
Marrying out to whites
Damn good black beans
But so what?
Damn good politics
But so what?
Oh there were times
Like in the orange groves
Outside Phoenix
My task was to mark charts
To ask the Guatemaltecas
When was your last period
And so on as they lined up
At the trailer to see a doctor

And that night in Harvard Yard
A North Vietnamese
Soldier-poet tested
Spanish he learned in Cuba
It worked
We found a third way
His voice a high wire
I crossed over to him
Fearless as a spider
If we didn't know a word
We filled in the blank
With a star
It is a light
That years later
I try not to curse

# Translation from the Vietnamese

for Kevin Bowen                    .

hold a poem up to the light
look for fractures
that make the crystal
the unburied bones
that make up his nightmares

knowing what cannot be healed
must be held
until it can be heard
above the detonations

in the crumpled silk of the jungle
a six-toned wood flute
the sound of one hand writing
down the worlds that survived

# Fragmentos/Fragments

*gracias a Teresa Márquez*

Escribo esta cartita en español
y es como conducir sin manos,
es como el sueño de volar,
un sentido de poder, el temor
de caer. Inglés. Mi máscara,
mi espada. En su lugar, este
kimono de palabras, este huipil.
Palabras que dejan que entra viento y
sol. Toco la seda, toco el algodón.
¿Quién es la mujer en el espejo?
Quiero conocerla.

I write this letter in Spanish, and it is
like driving without hands, a dream
of flight, a feeling of power, a fear
of falling. English. My mask, my
sword. In its place, this kimono of
words, this huipil. Words that let in
wind and sun. I touch the silk, the
cotton. Who is the woman in the
mirror? I want to know her.

Cada
palabra
que escribo
en español
es una luna

hole punched in the dark
with a pen

mi cara en
esta luz
mis ojos
mis labios
¿seré yo?

Each
word
I write
in Spanish
is a moon

hole punched in the dark
with a pen

my face
in this light
my eyes
my lips
is it really me?

Sometimes frightened,
I run back to the familiar
streets of English.

I go about my usual business,
making things go my way
at the bank, store, government office,

moving mountains in English
not by faith but by precision,
words aimed between eyes.

In moments of grace,
poetry or prayer,
English uses me.

But most of the time, I use it.
I do not always like what I
have become in this tongue.

Es distinto en español.
Escribo esta carta, paso a paso
por fe, en esta media luz,
algunas veces parando
para pedir direcciones.

Cuando no conozco una palabra
dejo un blank _____ así.
Llevo estos blanks conmigo
como velas hasta que alguien
me ayuda con un fósforo.
Y estas blanks
se transforman
en gotas de luz para guiarme
hasta que puedo dejar
las velas al lado del camino,
una ofrenda, una constelación
de sueños para los que siguen.

It is different in Spanish.
I write this letter, step by step,
by faith, in this half-light,
at times stopping
to ask for directions.

And when I don't know a word
I leave a blank _____ like this.
I carry these blanks with me
like candles until someone
stops to help, lights a match.
Emptiness giving way
to light that guides me
so that I can leave the candles
at the side of the road,
an offering, a constellation
of dreams for those who follow.

*Hablarte*
*en esta lengua*
*es como desnudarme*
*por la primera vez*
*ante tus ojos.*
*Temor, deseo,*
*sin volver . . .*

Speaking to you
in this tongue is like
undressing for the first time
before your eyes.
Fear, desire,
no turning back . . .

## Las Mañanitas

"Love, unpredictable as death" — Daisy Zamora
"It keeps you honest. It keeps you strange." — George Evans

The hour the world daubed

my forehead with sandalwood

mariachis accompanied me
to the graveyard
for the Day of the Dead

where cottonwood leaves
shimmered like jewels
in the navels of belly dancers

imagine the day
when we have a full day

pinto beans on jasmine rice

a rooster that does not know
what time it is
and tricks the sun
into staying over

the creak of a bed
like an orchestra warming up

# II. FIRST WORDS

## Untitled #2

You tell me there is a place
In the universe for those
Who wrestle with demons.
Tell me: What did the devil do
With my lost years?
Did he eat them?
Did he fall into a sound sleep
And so spare a single soul from pain?
I don't think so.
And why, all these years later,
Must I forgive him long enough
To touch with love
All that was lost?
Forgive myself long enough
To write these poems?

# Imperialism

The lady's British accent
was fake. Years later it still
infuriates. Her Cambridge estate
had china, flush toilets, English lessons.
In exchange for chores she taught me to speak
in full sentences, cured me of my accent,
a colored girl's dream, room and board.
She taught me to say what I mean.
Though to this day she refuses
to hear what I mean.

Ah, but she'd been round
the world, photographing
revolutions, toasting to Daniel
Ortega. She knew what was best
for a spic like me. Nightly
I recited Chaucer by her Greek
column and a peach tree

Miss, you tap the porcelain teapot.
Time for your nicotine fit.
Poof smoke away from my
face, but we're in the
same windowless room.
All I wanted was the vote,
the right to remain silent.
Now you call me ungrateful,
me, writing a new constitution
full of truth and bad grammar.

Trouble, trouble, educating
coloreds. Those years I picked
your tobacco and you botched
my lungs, you taught me to spell
trigger. Now I've got your gun.
Run Jane run, run run
Lady, dear lady,
the empire
is done.

# Wanted

*after Allen Ginsberg, 1988*

America our marriage is coming apart
I've done everything right got my degree
Now you tell me my English won't do
America I'm not good enough for you?
Better my Spanglish than your smooth talk America
No I won't sleep with you not now not ever
Ah come on America all I wanted was a little
   adobe house in Atrisco a porch swing
   two niños some democracy
Now I read in the *Albuquerque Journal* you left me
   for a younger woman
Bought drugs for guns     guns for drugs
Destroyed Managua in order to save it
Spied on communist Maryknoll nuns in Cleveland
America your face is on wanted posters in post offices
And I'm on sleeping pills again America
Last night I dreamed the Pentagon was a great
   Ouija board spelling out REPENT REPENT
In half sleep I reached for you love but got
   only a scent of amber waves of grain
I got up for a hit of caffeine the Book of Psalms
And whoosh I saw the promised land
You don't need citizenship papers there it's colored
   and smells of refried beans
Remember remember who you are America
Purple mountain majesty above fruited plains
   worked by mejicanos
America call off your dogs
America give me a green card though I don't qualify
America forgive me if I gag your memory
   at La Paloma bar on South Broadway
America I'm twenty-seven and tired thanks to you
And thanks to you I found God on a stoop on Arno Street
America you claim crime's fierce in this neighborhood
I tell you it's nothing next to your crimes
The wars we fund start at the package liquor store

and end twice a year at confession
America I don't want progress I want redemption
Cut the shit we could be lovers again don't hang up
America I'm your dark side embrace me and be saved
Pull yourself up by your bootstraps I know you can
America I'm not all bitter I'm a registered Republican
At parties when friends ask America who? I introduce
    you explain you've had a difficult upbringing
But I can't cover up for you America get that straight
Honey it's not too late it's not too late
America the ball's in your court now

# Sonogram

*para Raquel Dolores*

Little grasshopper
Heart popping like corn
Mexican jumping bean
Water drop sizzling on castiron of love and war
You immigrated from the cosmos
To this burning planet
Only to be detained by life
Your name written on greeting cards
And search warrants
Who's to say you will not grow up
Washing windshields, selling gum, eating fire
While a rich man's coffee cup lands on the table like a gavel?

Your birth will be one more cry severing the night

You are loved
You are the world's
You are not free

## Rally

Handsome as a stringed instrument

but your voice, with its aroma of wood smoke and rain
is pre-Columbian: a gourd full of seeds, a wood flute

when you say *justice* the word
is tough as a leek, true as Tewa

in a world where Wall Street memos
have obliterated the memory of corn
and a Brazilian tribe
that has no word for war

now clouds with their manes and black nostrils
tuned to the whip of your voice race south
hauling faxes, press releases

to a land where *la virgen de Guadalupe*
wears a Zapatista ski mask
and makes her appearance
on laptops in the Lacondón

hearing you, my shoulders ache
remembering when they were wings
I would speak too, but my truths emerge silently
in typos: Chiapaz, the z breaking out *peace*

a crowd moves like a ship beneath a sail of signs
silverfish microphones leap from the eddies
you lead the chant, "We are all Marcos"
I want to believe it is true: that we can become
the man/the woman whose mouth is an X
whose eyes circle our little world like planets
whose dreams are hot and black as good coffee
but with room for nutmeg and milk
space for even better dreams

you are far away again: I mail you these words
after this, no more poems about love
if a poem is not itself love it is noise
easy as carrying a sign
for the descendants of my ancestors, still landless

the hard work is the wait, the endless breathing
upon the brown egg held in our hands,
warming a world as breakable
as a rib at the end of a rifle butt
passing the egg from hand to hand to hand
until the quetzal's wings open
like cathedral doors

I have no proof
this day will come, all I can give you
is a sign, all I know is what
I have seen in my poems

## Meantimes

The questions catch us off guard,
a dust storm we drive through

Although headlights are powerless
against beating grit

You wonder if you want
me in the passenger seat

If the fights about stopping
and asking directions

Say something larger,
meaner about our journey

2.
A fog of newspapers between us,
horizons of headlines

Not even the obligatory remarks
about Rwanda, the weather

One day, who knows when,
our star died

Is the dark light now visible
to our disbelieving eyes?

3.
I offered you rosary beads
for the rearview mirror,
tear gas on a key ring

She would give you
an aerial view of your life,
a hammock of stars

4.
Can love be reset
like a bone?

Is the will a strong
enough splint?

Can we put in
another well?

When water tables
drop, is it forever?

5.
Do we have the courage
to let the questions hang
on a wire like *carne seca*

until the sun speaks
to us in the savory dryness?
Do we have the courage

to raise questions like children,
let them grow into
their own answers?

6.
Lightning breaks
the locks on our hearts

Thunder breaks into
the safe of night

Seed spills from bruised fruit,
as we wait for the sun

To reweave itself
across the loom of sky

## Discovering America

for P., 1992

*Santo Niño* on a
bedroom desk,
holy water in a
mouthwash bottle
Grandma had the
priest bless,
this house,
a medieval city
you visited,
what you sought
was not here.

Not in wrists
oiled with sage,
Chimayo earth
sprinkled on sheets,
nor San Felipe bells
that pecked away
the dark,
Cordova blanket
we hatched
awake in.

To prove love
I shed still
more centuries,
rung by rung
into a pueblo
kiva where
you touched
the *sipapu*,
canal the universe
emerged from,
brown baby glazed
in birth muds.

You thought
America

was on a map,
couldn't see it
in a woman,
olive skin,
silver loops
in lobes,
one for each
millennium
endured on this
husk of red earth,
this *nuevo méjico.*

Last night
I dreamed
a map of the
continent,
the train
that took you
from me whipped
across tracks
like a needle
on a seam
somewhere
near Canada.

It took me
four years
to heal.
Have you?
Have you
discovered
America
or at least
admitted
a woman grew
*maiz* here
long before
you named it
*corn?*

## Beauty Marks

I will not disguise
my love in a crossword puzzle,
my desire uses no pseudonym

the explosives I carry, I carry
in the open now,
not hidden in a nun's habit

Yet what we share
is invisible to the world

We are the air the world
breathes but cannot describe

the dark that knows it is dark
only by beauty marks of stars

# Only So Long

*Old Town Plaza, Albuquerque*

Castiron nights of August,
women refry beans, cicadas hum like
gourds on ankles of pueblo dancers.

Shop after shop,
mud walls fluted
as wasps' nests,

red chile pods
on doorposts
like Passover blood.

Pueblo women plant turquoise
on blankets under a portal,
harvest tourist dollars.

This night, my world,
your touch: I've learned
the names for so many things,

*come home,* I will give them all,
hundreds of days have poured
through my fingers like flour.

My patience is long
as a grocery list
but life is brief

as mesquite brush.
Someday, soon, I might
wrap up my wound and go.

## That Night

We set the clock back,
picked an hour from time's pockets

at sunrise boarded
our separate planes

love, for lack of another name

joy, promises
melted down to a cry

steel arrows
in a bloodied sky

# First Things

I am the blue woman
stroking a beaded earring
searching for the right song
at the red light
blue woman, 107 degrees, mesquite
trees fingering the winds
skirts of dust blown
back like Marilyn Monroe
I am the blue woman
wanting a new lipstick
some comprehension of Rwanda
an hour of silence
so cool and moist
melons happen, poems

Time now to feed the fish
lock doors, board a plane
I am the blue woman
who creates life
out of emergency exits, honeyed peanuts
the blue woman waits
the blue woman watches
the blue woman knows
her ground time will be brief.

# Afterword

My father's mother, María Jesús Martínez, used to call across town from her house in Albuquerque to say that she had been praying for me. A native of Chihuahua, Grandma had a rich Spanish accent that pressed hard against the narrow corridors of English, the passage she took to reach her numerous grandchildren. "Mijita," she would tell me, "I feel like the Lord wants you to read this verse from the Bible."

She often had me turn to the Book of Isaiah: "Moonlight will be bright as sunlight and sunlight itself be seven times brighter — like the light of seven days in one — on the day Yahweh dresses his people's wound and heals the scars of the blows they have received."

Light breaking forth from darkness, strangers that turn out to be angels, poor people inheriting the Earth while the rich are sent away empty — such were the images Grandma pondered in her marked-up Bible where scripture-study tracts written in Spanish were pressed between pages like roses.

Ironically, it was my grandmother's desire to read the Bible that led her away from Catholicism to a First Spanish Assembly of God congregation. It bothered her that laypeople were discouraged from reading scripture on their own; indeed, in those days reading the Bible at home was associated with Protestantism. Instead, María Jesús found new faith in a humble, cinder-block church where working-class Mexicans and Chicanos pored over the Good Book like scholars. Unlike Catholics, these people spoke to God without a priestly mediator. They prayed in tongues, languages not yet invented; and God answered back in the poetic cadences of a preacher who spoke Spanish, María Jesús's mother tongue.

I remember watching Grandma read her Bible at home. She often opened the book at random, letting her finger fall upon a verse. Stepping out of ordinary time and into mythic time, she read and re-read a few lines by the buttery light of her night lamp, extracting meanings, spinning new cosmologies.

In a magnificent paradox that anticipated Latin America's liberation theology, my grandmother dared to interpret her own life in light of a text that all too often had been used against the poor and against women. She named the sacred in experiences the world would never honor, namely cleaning, cooking, and caring for children and grandchildren. She survived the death of her husband knowing that in the end she belonged not to man but to God.

The documents that defined her were the Bible and her U.S. citizenship papers. But she pledged allegiance to one kingdom only, where she believed all people would be made welcome regardless of skin color or cash flow. Her reading freed her imagination. She saw a day when humanity would be made whole, when God would "heal the scars" of a world at war with itself.

Given the nature of my grandma's phone calls, it was inevitable that I would come to equate the written word with comfort, power, and magic. I began keeping a journal when I was about fourteen or fifteen years old. Slightly overweight and too shy to converse with most of my peers, I began conversing with myself in a green-and-white chemistry notebook. I wrote down accounts of the day, to-do lists, pep talks, and poems. I wrote my way out of depressions by copying down melancholic lyrics, then making up some of my own.

The notebook was a door between worlds temporal and eternal—a door too many writers close when they "grow up" and set out to learn something practical. I graduated from Princeton University in 1982 with a degree in public policy. There is little I recall about those years, but one image has stayed with me: I am sitting near a fountain by the Woodrow Wilson School of Public and International Affairs, reading the poet Nikki Giovanni. Four years into college, I am clear about one thing: Life is too short to work at a job that requires hose, heels, and forty hours a week. Why settle for a career when one might have a calling, I asked myself.

After graduation I returned to Albuquerque and joined what was then Sagrada Art School, a community headed by a Dominican nun and painter who warned budding artists to stay away from full-time jobs. I lived for about six years in Old Town, Albuquerque's original plaza, where Sagrada was located. A few doors away, the names of ancestors who had first settled in the plaza in 1706 were painted on a wall. I made it a habit to go to a restaurant or outdoor cafe and read first thing in the morning. I opened a book of poetry at random, waited for the caffeine to strike and for a stanza to reveal some secret of the universe. It always did, in imagery that was a far cry from that of supply and demand which I had tried learning at Princeton.

Whatever job I had—whether waiting on tables or freelance reporting—I did during the afternoons. In the mornings, with my poetry and my journal, I became my grandmother.

I came to depend upon my morning epiphanies, those visitations. The Holy Spirit? The muse? Who cared what name mankind had imposed upon the mystery of it all? I felt the joy of Jeremiah, the prophet María Jesús so often quoted—"When your words came, I devoured them: Your word was my delight and the joy of my heart."

From there it was an easy step, moving my pen across the page like the pointer of a Ouija board. Letter by letter, poem by poem, meanings were revealed. By 1987 I had finished a collection of poetry called Turning.

In 1988 my experience of poetry changed radically. That year the

U.S. government attempted to use one of my poems against me in a court of law. The poem, titled "Nativity, for Two Salvadoran Women," referred to the U.S. role in El Salvador's brutal civil war. The punch line of the poem was "In my country we sing of a baby in a manger, finance death squads."

Indicted on charges related to smuggling two refugee women into the country, I faced a twenty-five-year prison sentence. A year and a half earlier I had accompanied a Lutheran minister to the U.S.–Mexico border, where he helped two Salvadorans cross over as part of the Sanctuary movement.

The two women were pregnant, due to give birth in December. The minister, struck by the parallel with the story of the Holy Family fleeing oppression in Egypt, suggested I write an article about the women's plight. At the time I was covering religion for the *Albuquerque Journal* and freelancing for the *National Catholic Reporter*, an independent newsweekly.

The indictment lasted about seven months; then I went to trial along with the minister. It was a poet's nightmare, in which words, so full of liberating possibilities, were twisted and used against me and a movement dedicated to saving the lives of refugees. The nightmare penetrated even the thick adobe walls of my house; my attorney ordered me to be careful of what I said over the phone, given the likelihood of government spying.

Her worries were not so far-fetched. In the middle 1980s, the FBI spied on, among other groups, the Maryknoll nuns of Cleveland, who opposed U.S. military aid to Central America. At that time the United States was sending about $1.4 million a day to El Salvador alone.

After a two-week trial, I was acquitted on First Amendment grounds. The minister was also acquitted because we had taken our trip to the border in 1986—the year New Mexico had been declared a Sanctuary state by then-governor Toney Anaya.

After my acquittal, however, freedom of expression was more

of an abstraction for me than a reality. I felt as if someone had cut out my tongue. Writers, after all, talk in rough draft. Circumscribe what you say, and before long you are censoring what you write, however unwittingly. For years after the trial, I held emotions in check and treated language as if it were a tool to defend one's self or one's point of view — rather than a music, and writing an act of love on behalf of the self that can never be fully known or explained, much less condemned to either innocence or guilt.

Nonetheless, I continued struggling to write poetry. In 1990 I joined the staff of the *National Catholic Reporter* in Kansas City. Before long I was blaming my lack of creativity on the fact that I had a full-time job.

Then, in 1992, a miracle happened.

The poet and activist Luis Rodríguez invited me to a Chicano poetry festival at the Mexico Fine Arts Center in Chicago. I remember standing in the back of a dark auditorium and listening to various authors. The evening unfolded. Sandra Cisneros took her place and began reading from *Woman Hollering Creek*.

It was then, lost in the music of her words, that I heard a strange, dissonant note.

I heard a voice, a voice whose origins I've yet to name. These are the words I heard: "His nation chewed him up and spat him out like piñon shell and when he emerged from an airplane one late afternoon I knew I would one day make love with him."

A number of emotions vied for room in my heart at that moment, but fear prevailed. Somehow I knew that what I had heard belonged not to a poem but to a novel, a story I sensed was already finished and floating in its dark universe awaiting a ready ear and a blank page. The problem was that I had no idea how to write a novel; worse still, I didn't want to learn. I said to myself, go to bed, get a good night's sleep, by tomorrow morning you will have come to your senses.

The next morning, thankfully, I was still very much out of my mind. I felt ecstatic, yet deeply peaceful as I took out the hotel stationery and wrote down the words I'd heard the night before. My lack of formal training in the genre turned out to be a blessing. I could do nothing but sit still and listen. Nine months later I had completed a novel — or what I prefer to think of as a long poem in disguise about a Salvadoran refugee and his Chicana lover, titled *Mother Tongue*.

Years later, I was visited again; the first poems of *Breathing Between the Lines* came to me in a gust of joy one quiet afternoon in Cambridge, Massachusetts. For three months I lived inside that voice. When it ceased I continued to work in silence, editing what had come before and adding to the fold some poems written in prior years.

Maybe one day I will have the courage to believe that what I was following was my own voice — a voice free and whole, talking right over the heads of "the authorities," both real and imagined. In the land of poetry, such authorities are the ones who are sent away empty, for poetry belongs to the biblical meek whose inheritance is nothing less than the earth itself.

*About the Author*

Demetria Martínez's books include the widely
translated novel, *Mother Tongue* (Ballantine), winner
of a Western States Book Award for Fiction; two
books of poetry, *Breathing Between the Lines* and *The Devil's
Workshop* (University of Arizona Press); and *Confessions
of a Berlitz-Tape Chicana* (University of Oklahoma Press).
She writes a column for the *National Catholic Reporter,*
an independent progressive newsweekly and is an
immigrants' rights activist.

Mother Tongue is based in part upon her 1987–1988
federal indictment and trial in connection with the
alleged smuggling of Salvadoran refugees into the
United States as part of the Sanctuary Movement.
The charges, including conspiracy against the U.S.
government, carried a 25-year prison sentence.
Prosecutors tried to use her poetry against her during
the trial, which drew international attention. A
religion writer at the time covering the movement,
Martínez was acquitted on First Amendment grounds.
She resides in Albuquerque.